Baker's

SINCE 1780

A Passion for Chocolate

Baker's

SINCE 1780

®

A Passion for Chocolate

pil

Publications International, Ltd.

Favorite Brand Name Recipes at www.fbnr.com

Kraft Kitchens Manager: Mary Beth Harrington

Pictured on the front cover: Molten Chocolate Cake *(page 11)*.
Pictured on the back cover *(clockwise from top left):* Original BAKER'S® GERMAN'S® Sweet Chocolate Cake *(page 18)*, Rich 'N Thick Hot Chocolate *(page 86)* and Frozen German Sweet Chocolate Pie *(page 60)*.

ISBN-13: 978-1-4127-2799-0
ISBN-10: 1-4127-2799-5

Manufactured in China.

8 7 6 5 4 3 2 1

Microwave Cooking: Microwave ovens vary in wattage. Use the cooking times as guidelines and check for doneness before adding more time.

Preparation/Cooking Times: Preparation times are based on the approximate amount of time required to assemble the recipe before cooking, baking, chilling or serving. These times include preparation steps such as measuring, chopping and mixing. The fact that some preparations and cooking can be done simultaneously is taken into account. Preparation of optional ingredients and serving suggestions is not included.

Baker's
SINCE 1780

Celebrating our 225th Anniversary as America's Oldest Chocolate Brand

Contents

83

Presenting: *Chocolatier* Extraordinaire...

Chef Marcel

Chef Marcel Desaulniers is the executive chef of the Trellis Restaurant in Williamsburg, Va. A graduate of the Culinary Institute of America, Marcel has received several awards, including the James Beard Award for Outstanding Pastry Chef in America. This chocolate guru has written several books, most notably his Death by Chocolate series.

In honor of the 225th anniversary of Baker's Chocolate, I created this special chocolate cake. Whenever you make it—either for a birthday, special celebration, or dessert tonight—it is indeed festive!

The chocolaty fudge cake is two moist layers of fudge cake, covered not just with chocolate icing, but honest-to-goodness fudge icing—just the way my mom makes it. In fact, I designed this cake with her in mind. When I think of Mrs. D in the kitchen of our Rhode Island home, I can imagine her reaching for a box of Baker's Chocolate, with my five sisters and me waiting anxiously for whatever chocolate concoction she was creating. It's this combination of joyful memories and present-day chocolate passion that makes this chocolaty-smooth cake perfect for any occasion you choose.

After assembly, you may keep BAKER'S® 225th Anniversary Cake in the refrigerator for two to three days before serving. To avoid permeating the cake with refrigerator odors, place the cake in a large, tightly sealed plastic container.

America's Oldest Chocolate Brand

BAKER'S® 225th Anniversary Cake

Prep: 20 minutes • **Total:** 1 hour 54 minutes

- 2 teaspoons butter, melted, divided
- 1¾ cups flour
- ½ teaspoon baking soda
- ¼ teaspoon salt
- 1 package (8 squares) **BAKER'S** Semi-Sweet Baking Chocolate
- 1 cup (2 sticks) butter, cut into ½-inch pieces
- 1¼ cups sugar
- 3 large eggs
- ½ cup buttermilk
- 1 teaspoon vanilla
  BAKER'S® 225th Anniversary Fudge Icing (page 9)

PREHEAT oven to 325°F. Lightly grease 2 (9-inch) round cake pans with half of the melted butter. Cover the bottom of each pan with wax paper (or parchment paper); brush evenly with the remaining melted butter. Set aside.

SIFT together the flour, baking soda and salt; set aside. Place chocolate and the cut-up butter in a large microwaveable bowl. Microwave on HIGH 2 minutes or until the butter is melted. Stir until chocolate is completely melted; set aside.

BEAT the sugar and eggs in a medium bowl with an electric mixer on high speed 2 minutes or until slightly thickened and pale in color. Add the chocolate mixture; beat until well blended, about 15 seconds. Gradually add flour mixture, beating on low speed until well blended, about 1 minute. Scrape down the side of the bowl. Add buttermilk and vanilla; beat on low speed 15 seconds, then on medium speed an additional 15 seconds. (If batter is not completely blended at this point, mix by hand with a rubber spatula until mixture is well blended.) Pour the cake batter evenly into the prepared pans; spread with spatula, if necessary, to evenly cover the bottom of each pan.

  **America's Oldest Chocolate Brand**

BAKE on the middle oven rack 30 to 34 minutes or until toothpick inserted in centers comes out with fudgy crumbs. (Do not overbake.) Cool in pans 5 minutes. Remove from pans to wire racks; peel away and discard the paper. Cool completely. Fill and frost with **BAKER'S®** 225th Anniversary Fudge Icing. Refrigerate cake until ready to serve. Let stand at room temperature 30 minutes before serving.

Makes 16 servings

BAKER'S® 225th Anniversary Fudge Icing

Prep: 35 minutes • **Total:** 1 hour 35 minutes (includes refrigeration)

> 2 cups firmly packed dark brown sugar
>
> 1¼ cups heavy whipping cream
>
> 1 cup half-and-half
>
> 1 package (8 squares) **BAKER'S** Semi-Sweet Baking Chocolate, coarsely chopped
>
> 6 tablespoons butter, cut into ½-inch pieces

PLACE all ingredients except butter in a medium saucepan. Bring to a boil over medium heat, stirring frequently with wire whisk to dissolve the sugar and melt the chocolate. Reduce heat to medium-low; simmer 25 minutes or until thickened, stirring frequently.

REMOVE from heat. Add the butter, one piece at a time, stirring after each addition until it is completely melted before adding the next piece. Pour the fudge mixture into 15×10×1-inch pan and spread evenly. Refrigerate at least 1 hour. (If refrigerating for more than 1 hour, let stand at room temperature 20 minutes before beating as directed in next step.)

PLACE chilled fudge mixture in a large bowl and beat with an electric mixer on high speed 1 minute; scrape the bottom and side of the bowl. Continue beating 30 seconds or until light and fluffy. Immediately frost the cake. *Makes 5¾ cups*

Baker's
SINCE 1780

Show Stoppers

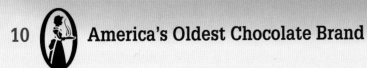

Molten Chocolate Cakes

Prep: 15 minutes • **Bake:** 16 minutes • **Total:** 31 minutes

- 1 package (8 squares) **BAKER'S** Semi-Sweet Baking Chocolate
- 1 cup (2 sticks) butter
- 2 cups powdered sugar
- ¾ cup flour
- 5 whole eggs
- 4 egg yolks
  Powdered sugar and raspberries, optional

PREHEAT oven to 425°F. Grease 8 (6-ounce) custard cups or souffle dishes. Place on baking sheet.

MICROWAVE chocolate and butter in large microwaveable bowl on HIGH 2 minutes or until butter is melted. Stir with wire whisk until chocolate is completely melted. Add powdered sugar and flour; mix well. Add whole eggs and egg yolks; stir until well blended. Pour batter evenly into prepared custard cups.

BAKE 15 to 16 minutes or until cakes are firm around edges but soft in the centers. Let stand 1 minute. Run small metal spatula around cakes to loosen. Carefully invert cakes onto dessert dishes. Sprinkle lightly with additional powdered sugar and raspberries, if desired. Serve warm.   ***Makes 16 servings, ½ cake each***

did you know...

In 1833, Baker's Cocoa was the only packaged and branded food product sold in the small general store co-owned by Abraham Lincoln in Old Salem, Illinois.

Awesome Sundae Pie

Prep: 20 minutes
Total: 3 hours 20 minutes (includes refrigeration and freezing)

   6 squares **BAKER'S** Semi-Sweet Baking Chocolate
   1 tablespoon butter or margarine
   ¾ cup finely chopped **PLANTERS** Pecans, toasted
   ¾ cup **BAKER'S ANGEL FLAKE** Coconut
   1 quart (4 cups) ice cream, any flavor, softened
   1 cup thawed **COOL WHIP** Whipped Topping
   3 maraschino cherries

LINE 9-inch pie plate with foil; lightly grease foil. Microwave chocolate and butter in large microwaveable bowl on HIGH 1½ minutes or until butter is melted, stirring after 1 minute. Stir until chocolate is completely melted. Stir in pecans and coconut. Spread evenly onto bottom and up side of prepared pie plate.

REFRIGERATE 1 hour or until firm. Lift crust out of pie plate. Carefully peel off foil. Return crust to pie plate or place on serving plate. Fill with scoops of the ice cream; cover.

FREEZE 2 hours or until firm. Top with whipped topping and cherries just before serving. Store leftover pie in freezer.

Makes 8 servings

Tip: Before serving, remove pie from freezer. Let stand at room temperature 10 minutes to allow pie to soften slightly for easier cutting.

America's Oldest Chocolate Brand

Chocolate Bliss Cheesecake

Prep: 30 minutes • **Bake:** 1 hour
Total: 5 hours 30 minutes (includes refrigeration)

- 18 **OREO** Chocolate Sandwich Cookies, finely crushed (about 1½ cups)
- 2 tablespoons butter or margarine, melted
- 3 packages (8 ounces each) **PHILADELPHIA** Cream Cheese, softened
- ¾ cup sugar
- 1 teaspoon vanilla
- 1 package (8 squares) **BAKER'S** Semi-Sweet Baking Chocolate, melted, slightly cooled
- 3 eggs

  Cocoa powder and powdered sugar, optional

PREHEAT oven to 325°F if using a silver 9-inch springform pan, or to 300°F if using a dark, nonstick 9-inch springform pan. Mix cookie crumbs and butter; press firmly onto bottom of pan.

BEAT cream cheese, sugar and vanilla in large bowl with electric mixer on medium speed until well blended. Add melted chocolate; mix well. Add eggs, 1 at a time, mixing on low speed after each addition just until blended. Pour over crust.

BAKE 55 minutes to 1 hour or until center is almost set. Run knife or metal spatula around rim of pan to loosen cake; cool before removing rim of pan. Refrigerate 4 hours or overnight. Dust top of cheesecake with cocoa powder. Top with a heart-shaped stencil and sprinkle with powdered sugar, if desired. Store leftover cheesecake in refrigerator. ***Makes 12 servings***

  **America's Oldest Chocolate Brand**

White Chocolate Mousse

Prep: 10 minutes
Total: 2 hours 30 minutes (includes refrigeration)

    1 package (6 squares) **BAKER'S**
         Premium White Baking Chocolate
    1½ cups whipping cream, divided

MICROWAVE chocolate and ¼ cup of the whipping cream in large microwaveable bowl on HIGH 2 minutes or until chocolate is almost melted, stirring after 1 minute. Stir until chocolate is completely melted. Cool 20 minutes or to room temperature, stirring occasionally.

BEAT remaining 1¼ cups whipping cream in chilled medium bowl with electric mixer on medium speed until soft peaks form. (Do not overbeat.) Add half of the whipped cream to chocolate mixture; stir gently with wire whisk until well blended. Add remaining whipped cream; stir just until blended. Pour into 6 individual dessert dishes or small serving bowl.

REFRIGERATE at least 2 hours or until firm. Store leftover dessert in refrigerator.

Makes 6 servings, about ½ cup each

Tip: Top with a sliced strawberry just before serving.

Original BAKER'S® GERMAN'S® Sweet Chocolate Cake

Prep: 30 minutes • **Bake:** 30 minutes
Total: 2 hours (includes cooling)

1 package (4 ounces) **BAKER'S GERMAN'S**
   Sweet Chocolate

½ cup water

2 cups flour

1 teaspoon baking soda

¼ teaspoon salt

1 cup (2 sticks) butter, softened

2 cups sugar

4 eggs, separated

1 teaspoon vanilla

1 cup buttermilk

Coconut-Pecan Filling and Frosting (page 84)

PREHEAT oven to 350°F. Cover bottoms of 3 (9-inch) round cake pans with wax paper; grease sides of pans. Microwave chocolate and water in large microwaveable bowl on HIGH 1½ to 2 minutes or until chocolate is almost melted, stirring after 1 minute. Stir until chocolate is completely melted.

MIX flour, baking soda and salt; set aside. Beat butter and sugar in large bowl with electric mixer on medium speed until light and fluffy. Add egg yolks, 1 at a time, beating well after each addition. Blend in melted chocolate and vanilla. Add flour mixture alternately with the buttermilk, beating until well blended after each addition.

BEAT egg whites in small bowl with electric mixer on high speed until stiff peaks form. Gently stir into batter. Pour evenly into prepared pans.

 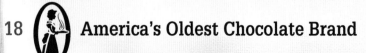 **America's Oldest Chocolate Brand**

BAKE 30 minutes or until toothpick inserted in centers comes out clean. Immediately run small metal spatula around cake layers in pans. Cool in pans 15 minutes; remove layers from pans to wire racks. Remove and discard wax paper. Cool cake layers completely. Spread Coconut-Pecan Filling and Frosting between cake layers and onto top of cake. ***Makes 16 servings***

Chocolate Plunge

Prep: 5 minutes • **Total:** 5 minutes

⅔ cup light corn syrup

½ cup whipping cream

1 package (8 squares) **BAKER'S**
Semi-Sweet Baking Chocolate

MICROWAVE corn syrup and whipping cream in large microwaveable bowl on HIGH 1½ minutes or until mixture comes to boil. Add chocolate; stir until completely melted.

SERVE warm as a dip with strawberries, pretzels, pound cake cubes and pineapple pieces.

Makes 12 servings, 2 tablespoons each

Tip: To make **Chocolate-Peanut Butter Plunge,** prepare as directed, stirring in ½ cup peanut butter with the chocolate. For **Chocolate-Raspberry Plunge,** prepare as directed, stirring in ¼ cup seedless raspberry jam with the chocolate. For **Mocha Plunge,** prepare as directed, stirring in 1 tablespoon **MAXWELL HOUSE** Instant Coffee granules with the chocolate.

Chocolate-Dipped Delights

Prep: 15 minutes • **Total:** 45 minutes

> 1 package (4 ounces) **BAKER'S GERMAN'S** Sweet Chocolate
>
> Assorted dippers, such as pretzel rods, whole strawberries, dried apricots or pineapple pieces

MICROWAVE chocolate in small microwaveable bowl on HIGH 1½ minutes or until chocolate is almost melted, stirring after 1 minute. Stir until chocolate is completely melted.

DIP assorted dippers into chocolate; let excess chocolate drip off.

LET stand at room temperature or refrigerate on wax paper-lined baking sheet 30 minutes, or until chocolate is firm.   ***Makes 10 servings***

did you know...

When Baker's Chocolate was first introduced in the pre-Revolutionary days, it was not used for baking. Rather, those in the Boston area would purchase the "hard cakes" and scrape the chocolate into boiled water to make a sweetened chocolate drink.

Chocolate-Dipped Apples

Prep: 10 minutes
Total: 40 minutes (includes refrigeration)

- 6 wooden pop sticks
- 6 small to medium apples, washed and well dried
- 1 tub (7 ounces) **BAKER'S** Dipping Chocolate, any variety
- ¾ cup **PLANTERS** Chopped Pecans

INSERT 1 wooden pop stick into stem end of each apple.

MICROWAVE chocolate as directed on package. Dip bottom half of each apple into chocolate, turning until evenly coated. Sprinkle pecans over chocolate. Place on wax paper-covered tray.

REFRIGERATE 30 minutes or until chocolate is firm. Cut each apple in half to serve. Cover and store any leftover uncut apples in refrigerator.

Makes 6 apples or 12 servings, ½ apple each

Tip: Substitute **BAKER'S ANGEL FLAKE** Coconut, chopped **PLANTER'S COCKTAIL** Peanuts or chopped **OREO** Chocolate Sandwich Cookies for the pecans.

BAKER'S® Chocolate Holiday Bark

Prep: 20 minutes
Total: 1 hour 20 minutes (includes refrigeration)

- 1 package (8 squares) **BAKER'S** Semi-Sweet Baking Chocolate, chopped
- 1 package (6 squares) **BAKER'S** Premium White Baking Chocolate, chopped
- 1 cup **PLANTERS** Almonds, toasted
- ½ cup dried cranberries
- ½ cup chopped dried apricots

MICROWAVE semi-sweet chocolate and white chocolate in separate medium microwaveable bowls as directed on packages. Add half each of the almonds, cranberries and apricots to each chocolate; stir until well blended.

DROP spoonfuls of the chocolate mixtures onto wax paper-covered baking sheet, alternating the colors of chocolates. Cut through chocolate mixtures with a knife several times for marble effect.

REFRIGERATE at least 1 hour or until firm. Break into 24 pieces. Store in tightly covered container at room temperature.   *Makes 24 servings*

*Tip: Substitute 1 cup coarsely chopped **OREO** Chocolate Sandwich Cookies or candied citrus for the almonds or mixed dried fruit.*

  America's Oldest Chocolate Brand

Bittersweet Chocolate Truffles

Prep: 15 minutes
Total: 2 hours 15 minutes (includes refrigeration)

> 2 packages (6 squares each) **BAKER'S** Bittersweet Baking Chocolate
>
> ¾ cup whipping cream
>
> 3 tablespoons granulated sugar
>
> 1 tablespoon butter or margarine
>
> 1 teaspoon vanilla
>
> ½ cup powdered sugar

MICROWAVE chocolate, whipping cream, granulated sugar and butter in large microwaveable bowl on HIGH 2 minutes or until whipping cream is simmering. Add vanilla; stir until chocolate is completely melted and mixture is well blended.

REFRIGERATE 2 hours or until mixture is firm enough to handle.

SCOOP truffle mixture with melon baller or teaspoon, then roll into 24 balls, each about 1½ inches in diameter. Roll in powdered sugar until evenly coated. Store in tightly covered container in refrigerator.

Makes 2 dozen truffles or 12 servings, 2 truffles each

Tip: *Truffles can be prepared up to 3 weeks ahead for gift giving. Store between layers of wax paper in tightly covered container in refrigerator. For a variation, roll truffles in unsweetened cocoa powder,* **BAKER'S ANGEL FLAKE** *Coconut or finely chopped* **PLANTER'S** *Pecans.*

Caramel-Pecan Brownies

Prep: 20 minutes • **Bake:** 55 minutes • **Total:** 1 hour 15 minutes

4 squares **BAKER'S** Unsweetened Baking Chocolate

¾ cup (1½ sticks) butter or margarine

2 cups sugar

4 eggs

1 cup flour

1 bag (14 ounces) **KRAFT** Caramels

⅓ cup whipping cream

2 cups **PLANTERS** Pecan Halves, divided

PREHEAT oven to 350°F. Line 13×9-inch baking pan with foil, with ends extending over sides of pan. Generously grease foil.

MICROWAVE chocolate and butter in large microwaveable bowl on HIGH 2 minutes or until butter is melted. Stir until chocolate is completely melted. Stir in sugar until well blended. Add eggs; mix well. Stir in flour until well blended. Spread half of the batter into prepared pan.

BAKE 25 minutes or until top is firm to the touch. Meanwhile, microwave caramels and whipping cream in medium microwaveable bowl on HIGH 2 minutes or until caramels begin to melt. Stir until caramels are completely melted. Stir in 1 cup of the pecan halves.

SPREAD caramel mixture evenly over brownie; top with remaining brownie batter. (Some caramel mixture may peek through.) Sprinkle with remaining 1 cup pecan halves. Bake an additional 30 minutes or until top is firm to the touch. Cool in pan on wire rack. Using foil handles, remove brownies from pan. Cut into 32 squares. Store in tightly covered container at room temperature. *Makes 32 servings*

Chocolate-Dipped Coconut Macaroons

Prep: 15 minutes • **Bake:** 20 minutes
Total: 1 hour 35 minutes (includes cooling)

- 1 package (14 ounces) **BAKER'S ANGEL FLAKE** Coconut (5⅓ cups)
- ⅔ cup sugar
- 6 tablespoons flour
- ¼ teaspoon salt
- 4 egg whites, lightly beaten
- 1 teaspoon almond extract
- 1 package (8 squares) **BAKER'S** Semi-Sweet Baking Chocolate, melted

PREHEAT oven to 325°F. Mix coconut, sugar, flour and salt in large bowl until well blended. Add egg whites and almond extract; mix well. Drop by tablespoonfuls, 2 inches apart, onto greased and floured baking sheets.

BAKE 20 minutes or until edges of cookies are golden brown. Immediately remove from baking sheets to wire racks. Cool completely.

DIP cookies halfway into melted chocolate. Let stand at room temperature or refrigerate on wax paper-lined tray 30 minutes or until chocolate is firm.

Makes about 3 dozen cookies or 36 servings, 1 cookie each

Tip: Store in tightly covered container at room temperature for up to 1 week.

Chocolate-Dipped Strawberries

Prep: 10 minutes
Total: 40 minutes (includes refrigeration)

  1 package (7 ounces) **BAKER'S** Real
      Milk Dipping Chocolate
36 medium strawberries

MELT chocolate as directed on package.

DIP strawberries into chocolate; let excess chocolate drip off.

LET stand at room temperature or refrigerate on wax paper-covered baking sheet or tray 30 minutes or until chocolate is firm. For best results, serve strawberries the same day they are prepared.

*Makes 3 dozen dipped strawberries or
18 servings, 2 strawberries each*

Tip: *For a variation, prepare as directed, using **BAKER'S** Real Dark Semi-Sweet Dipping Chocolate or 7 ounces melted **BAKER'S** **GERMAN'S** Sweet Chocolate for the dipping chocolate.*

Easy Chocolate-Caramel Popcorn

Prep: 15 minutes • **Bake:** 20 minutes
Total: 1 hour 5 minutes

  1 bag (14 ounces) **KRAFT** Caramels
  3 tablespoons butter or margarine
  2 tablespoons water
12 cups air-popped popcorn
  1 cup **PLANTERS COCKTAIL** Peanuts
  4 squares **BAKER'S** Semi-Sweet Baking Chocolate, finely chopped

PREHEAT oven to 300°F. Microwave caramels, butter and water in large microwaveable bowl on HIGH 2½ to 3 minutes or until caramels are completely melted, stirring after each minute.

COMBINE popcorn and peanuts in large bowl. Drizzle with the caramel mixture; toss to evenly coat. Spread onto greased large baking sheet.

BAKE 20 minutes, stirring after 10 minutes. Sprinkle with chocolate; toss using 2 spoons until well mixed. Spread onto sheet of wax paper; cool completely. Break apart into small clusters or individual pieces. Store in tightly covered container at room temperature for up to 1 week.   ***Makes 18 servings, about ¾ cup each***

Tip: To melt caramels on the stove, place caramels, butter and water in heavy saucepan. Cook on low heat until caramels are completely melted, stirring frequently.

Peanut Butter Oatmeal Chocolate Chunk Cookies

Prep: 15 minutes • **Bake:** 13 minutes
Total: 28 minutes

1	cup flour
1	cup old-fashioned or quick-cooking oats
½	teaspoon baking soda
½	teaspoon **CALUMET** Baking Powder
¼	teaspoon salt
½	cup granulated sugar
½	cup firmly packed brown sugar
½	cup (1 stick) margarine, softened
½	cup peanut butter
1	egg
1½	teaspoons vanilla
6	squares **BAKER'S** Semi-Sweet Baking Chocolate, coarsely chopped

PREHEAT oven to 375°F. Mix flour, oats, baking soda, baking powder and salt; set aside.

BEAT sugars, margarine and peanut butter in large bowl with electric mixer on medium speed until light and fluffy. Add egg and vanilla; mix well. Gradually add flour mixture, mixing until well blended after each addition. Stir in chopped chocolate. Drop heaping tablespoonfuls of dough, 2 inches apart, onto ungreased baking sheets.

BAKE 12 to 13 minutes or until lightly browned. Cool 1 minute; remove from baking sheets to wire racks. Cool completely.

Makes 2½ dozen cookies or 30 servings, 1 cookie each

Chocolate Bliss Caramel Brownies

Prep: 20 minutes • **Bake:** 35 minutes • **Total:** 55 minutes

4	squares **BAKER'S** Unsweetened Baking Chocolate
¾	cup (1½ sticks) butter or margarine
2	cups sugar
4	eggs
1	cup flour
1	cup chopped **PLANTERS** Pecans or Walnuts
25	**KRAFT** Caramels (½ of 14-ounce bag)
2	tablespoons milk
1	package (12 ounces) **BAKER'S** Semi-Sweet Chocolate Chunks

PREHEAT oven to 350°F. Line 13×9-inch baking pan with foil, with ends extending over sides of pan. Grease foil.

PLACE chocolate squares and butter in large microwaveable bowl. Microwave on HIGH 2 minutes or until butter is melted. Stir until chocolate is completely melted. Add sugar; mix well. Blend in eggs. Add flour; mix well. Stir in pecans. Spread into prepared pan.

BAKE 30 to 35 minutes or until toothpick inserted in center comes out with fudgy crumbs. (Do not overbake.)

MEANWHILE, place caramels and milk in microwaveable bowl. Microwave on HIGH 2 minutes, stirring after 1 minute. Stir until caramels are completely melted and mixture is well blended. Gently spread over brownie in pan; sprinkle with chocolate chunks. Cool in pan on wire rack. Using foil handles, lift brownies from pan. Cut into 36 squares. Store in tightly covered container at room temperature. ***Makes 36 servings***

SINCE 1780

Baker's®

Easy One Bowl Favorites

One Bowl Recipe

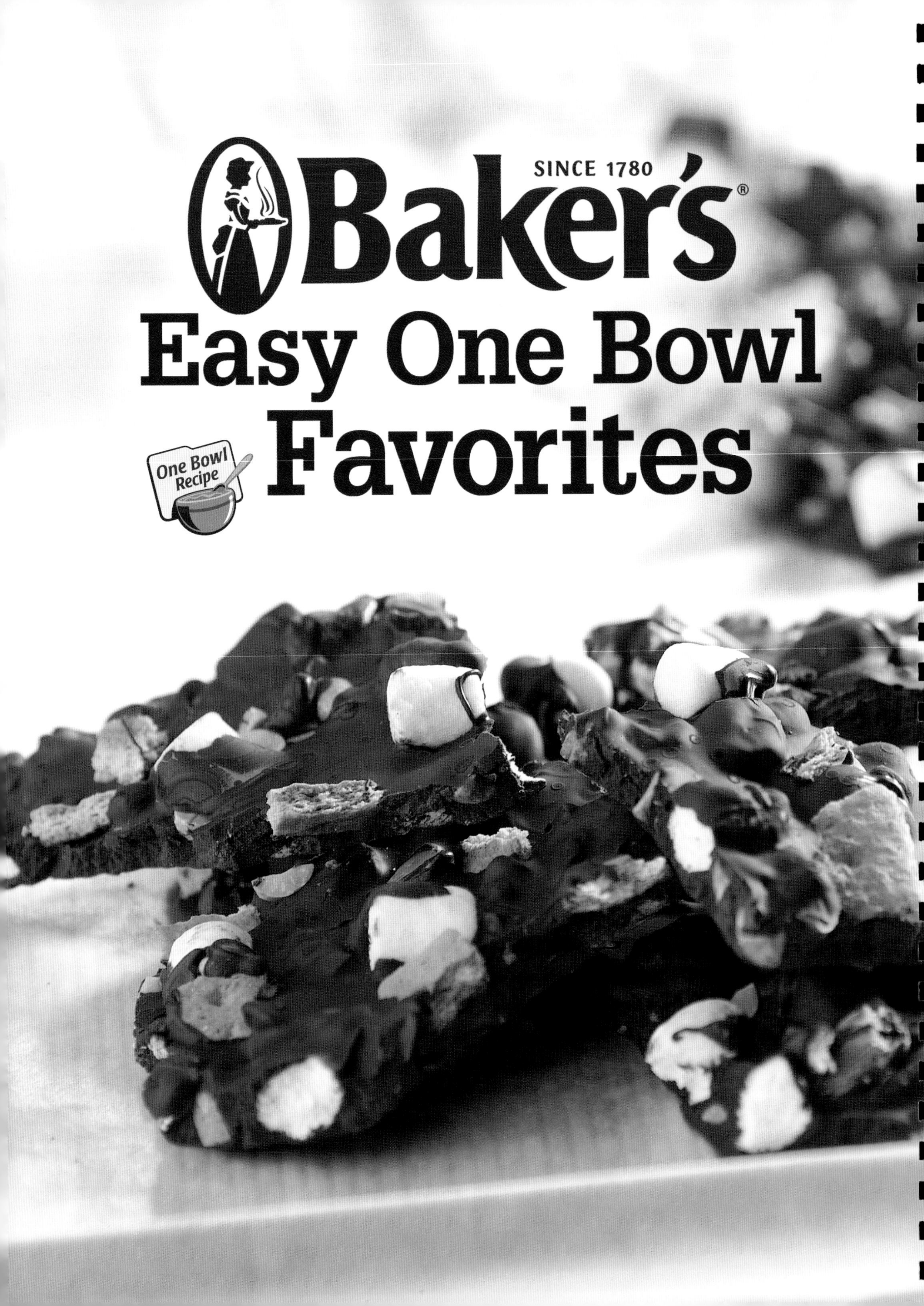

BAKER'S® ONE BOWL
Rocky Road Chocolate Bark

Prep: 20 minutes
Total: 1 hour 20 minutes (includes refrigeration)

- 1½ packages (12 squares) **BAKER'S** Semi-Sweet Baking Chocolate
- ⅓ cup chopped **PLANTERS** Dry Roasted Peanuts
- ⅓ cup coarsely broken **HONEY MAID** Honey Grahams
- ⅓ cup **JET-PUFFED** Miniature Marshmallows

MICROWAVE chocolate in medium microwaveable bowl on HIGH 2 minutes or until chocolate is almost melted, stirring after 1 minute. Stir until chocolate is completely melted.

ADD remaining ingredients; mix well. Spread onto wax paper-covered baking sheet or tray.

REFRIGERATE 1 hour or until firm. Break into 10 pieces. Store in tightly covered container at room temperature. ***Makes 10 servings***

did you know...

The former Administration Building of Walter Baker & Company in Dorchester, Mass., still houses a replica of the *La Belle Chocolatiere* painting. In addition, the roof still holds the giant neon sign that once illuminated the area with the words "Walter Baker."

BAKER'S® ONE BOWL
Chocolate-Strawberry Cake

Prep: 15 minutes • **Bake:** 30 minutes
Total: 1 hour 45 minutes (includes cooling)

- 5 squares **BAKER'S** Semi-Sweet Baking Chocolate, divided
- 6 tablespoons butter or margarine
- ¾ cup sugar
- 1 teaspoon vanilla
- 2 eggs
- 1¼ cups flour, divided
- ½ teaspoon baking soda
- ¾ cup water
- 1½ cups thawed **COOL WHIP** Whipped Topping
- 1 cup sliced strawberries

PREHEAT oven to 350°F. Place 3 of the chocolate squares and the butter in large microwaveable bowl. Microwave on HIGH 2 minutes or until butter is melted. Stir until chocolate is completely melted.

STIR in sugar and vanilla until well blended. Add eggs, 1 at a time, beating with electric mixer on low speed after each addition until well blended. Add ¼ cup of the flour and the baking soda; mix well. Add remaining 1 cup flour alternately with the water, beating until well blended after each addition. Pour evenly into 9-inch round cake pan sprayed with cooking spray.

BAKE 30 minutes or until toothpick inserted in center comes out clean. Cool in pan 10 minutes; remove from pan to wire rack. Cool completely. Top with the whipped topping and

strawberries just before serving. Melt remaining 2 chocolate squares as directed on package; drizzle over cake. Let stand until chocolate is set. Store in refrigerator.

Makes 10 servings

America's Oldest Chocolate Brand 45

BAKER'S® ONE BOWL
Chocolate Swirl
Cheesecake

Prep: 10 minutes • **Bake:** 40 minutes
Total: 3 hours 50 minutes (includes refrigeration)

- 4 squares **BAKER'S** Semi-Sweet Baking Chocolate
- 2 packages (8 ounces each) **PHILADELPHIA** Cream Cheese, softened, divided
- ½ cup sugar, divided
- 2 eggs, divided
- 1 **OREO** Pie Crust (6-ounce)
- ½ teaspoon vanilla

PREHEAT oven to 350°F. Microwave chocolate in large microwaveable bowl on HIGH 1½ minutes or until chocolate is almost melted, stirring every 30 seconds. Stir until chocolate is completely melted. Add 1 package of the cream cheese, ¼ cup of the sugar and 1 of the eggs; beat with wire whisk until well blended. Pour into crust.

BEAT remaining package of cream cheese, remaining ¼ cup sugar, remaining egg and the vanilla in same bowl with wire whisk until well blended. Spoon over chocolate batter. Cut through batter with knife several times for marble effect.

BAKE 40 minutes or until center is almost set. Cool. Refrigerate 3 hours or overnight. Let stand at room temperature 20 minutes before serving. Store leftover cheesecake in refrigerator.

Makes 8 servings

BAKER'S® ONE BOWL Brownies

Prep: 15 minutes • **Bake:** 35 minutes • **Total:** 50 minutes

    4 squares **BAKER'S** Unsweetened Baking Chocolate
    ¾ cup (1½ sticks) butter or margarine
    2 cups sugar
    3 eggs
    1 teaspoon vanilla
    1 cup flour
    1 cup coarsely chopped **PLANTERS** Pecans

PREHEAT oven to 350°F. Line 13×9-inch baking pan with foil, with ends extending over sides of pan. Grease foil.

MICROWAVE chocolate and butter in large microwaveable bowl on HIGH 2 minutes or until butter is melted. Stir until chocolate is completely melted. Stir in sugar. Blend in eggs and vanilla. Add flour and pecans; mix well. Spread into prepared pan.

BAKE 30 to 35 minutes or until toothpick inserted in center comes out with fudgy crumbs. (Do not overbake.) Cool in pan on wire rack. Using foil handles, remove brownies from pan. Cut into 24 squares. Store in tightly covered container at room temperature.   ***Makes 24 servings***

Tip: For **Cake-Like Brownies**, *prepare as directed, stirring in ½ cup milk along with the eggs and vanilla, and increasing flour to 1½ cups. For* **Extra-Thick Brownies,** *prepare batter as directed; spreading into 9-inch square baking pan. Bake 50 minutes. Cool, then cut into 16 squares. For* **Extra-Fudgy Brownies**, *prepare as directed, using 4 eggs.*

America's Oldest Chocolate Brand

BAKER'S® ONE BOWL
Chocolate Fudge

Prep: 10 minutes
Total: 2 hours 10 minutes (includes refrigeration)

- 2 packages (8 squares each) **BAKER'S** Semi-Sweet Baking Chocolate
- 1 can (14 ounces) sweetened condensed milk
- 2 teaspoons vanilla
- 1 cup chopped **PLANTERS** Walnuts

LINE 8-inch square pan with foil, with ends extending over sides of pan. Set aside. Microwave chocolate and milk in large microwaveable bowl on HIGH 2 to 3 minutes or until chocolate is almost melted, stirring after 2 minutes. Stir until chocolate is completely melted. Blend in vanilla. Stir in walnuts.

SPREAD into prepared pan.

REFRIGERATE 2 hours or until firm. Using foil handles, lift fudge from pan. Cut into 48 pieces.

*Makes 4 dozen pieces or 24 servings,
2 pieces each*

Tip: For a flavor variation, substitute toasted **BAKER'S ANGEL FLAKE** Coconut for the chopped walnuts. To make **Peanut Butter Fudge**, prepare as directed. Omit the walnuts and spread into prepared pan. Immediately drop ½ cup peanut butter by teaspoonfuls over fudge; cut through peanut butter with knife several times for marble effect. Refrigerate as directed.

  **America's Oldest Chocolate Brand**

BAKER'S® ONE BOWL
Chocolate Bliss Cookies

Prep: 15 minutes • **Bake:** 13 minutes
Total: 28 minutes

>   2   packages (8 squares each) **BAKER'S**
>   Semi-Sweet Baking Chocolate, divided
>   ¾   cup firmly packed brown sugar
>   ¼   cup (½ stick) butter, slightly softened
>   2   eggs
>   1   teaspoon vanilla
>   ½   cup flour
>   ¼   teaspoon **CALUMET** Baking Powder
>   2   cups chopped **PLANTERS** Walnuts

PREHEAT oven to 350°F. Coarsely chop 8 of the chocolate squares; set aside. Microwave remaining 8 chocolate squares in large microwaveable bowl on HIGH 2 minutes, stirring after 1 minute. Stir until chocolate is completely melted. Add brown sugar, butter, eggs and vanilla; stir until well blended. Add flour and baking powder; mix well. Stir in chopped chocolate and walnuts. (Note: If omitting nuts, increase flour to ¾ cup to prevent excessive spreading of cookies as they bake.)

DROP rounded tablespoonfuls of dough, 2 inches apart, onto ungreased baking sheets.

BAKE 12 to 13 minutes or until cookies are puffed and shiny. Cool 1 minute; remove from baking sheets to wire racks. Cool completely.

Makes 2½ dozen cookies or 30 servings,
1 cookie each

America's Oldest Chocolate Brand

BAKER'S® ONE BOWL
Cream Cheese Brownies

Prep: 15 minutes • **Bake:** 40 minutes • **Total:** 55 minutes

4	squares **BAKER'S** Unsweetened Baking Chocolate
¾	cup (1½ sticks) butter
2½	cups sugar, divided
5	eggs, divided
1¼	cups flour, divided
1	package (8 ounces) **PHILADELPHIA** Cream Cheese, softened

PREHEAT oven to 350°F. Line 13×9-inch baking pan with foil, with ends extending over sides of pan. Grease foil.

MICROWAVE chocolate and butter in large microwaveable bowl on HIGH 2 minutes or until butter is melted. Stir until chocolate is completely melted. Add 2 cups of the sugar; stir until well blended. Add 4 of the eggs; mix well. Stir in 1 cup of the flour until well blended. Spread batter into prepared pan.

BEAT cream cheese, remaining ½ cup sugar, remaining egg and remaining ¼ cup flour in same bowl with wire whisk until well blended. Spoon over brownie batter. Cut through cream cheese mixture with knife several times for marble effect.

BAKE 35 to 40 minutes or until toothpick inserted in center comes out with fudgy crumbs. (Do not overbake.) Cool in pan on wire rack. Using foil handles, lift brownies from pan. Cut into 32 squares. Store leftover brownies, covered, in refrigerator.

Makes 32 servings

BAKER'S® ONE BOWL
Midnight Bliss Cake

Prep: 10 minutes • **Bake:** 1 hour • **Total:** 1 hour 10 minutes

- 1 package (2-layer size) chocolate cake mix, any variety
- 1 package (4-serving size) **JELL-O** Chocolate Flavor Instant Pudding & Pie Filling
- ½ cup **GENERAL FOODS INTERNATIONAL**, any coffee flavor
- 4 eggs
- 1 container (8 ounces) **BREAKSTONE'S** or **KNUDSEN** Sour Cream
- ½ cup vegetable oil
- ½ cup water
- 1 package (8 squares) **BAKER'S** Semi-Sweet Baking Chocolate, chopped

  Powdered sugar, optional

PREHEAT oven to 350°F. Lightly grease 12-cup fluted tube pan or 10-inch tube pan; set aside.

BEAT all ingredients except chopped chocolate in large bowl with electric mixer on low speed just until moistened, stopping frequently to scrape side of bowl. Beat on medium speed 2 minutes or until well blended. Stir in chopped chocolate. Spoon into prepared pan.

BAKE 50 minutes to 1 hour or until toothpick inserted near center comes out clean. Cool in pan 10 minutes. Loosen cake from side of pan with spatula or knife. Invert cake onto wire rack; gently remove pan. Cool completely. Lightly sprinkle with powdered sugar just before serving, if desired.

Makes 18 servings

America's Oldest Chocolate Brand

Tip: For a flavor variation, substitute 2 tablespoons **MAXWELL HOUSE** Instant Coffee for the $\frac{1}{2}$ cup **GENERAL FOODS INTERNATIONAL**.

Baker's
SINCE 1780
Classic
Chocolate
Recipes

Easy Cookie Bars

Prep: 15 minutes • **Bake:** 30 minutes • **Total:** 45 minutes

½ cup (1 stick) butter or margarine, melted

1½ cups **HONEY MAID** Graham Cracker Crumbs

1⅓ cups **BAKER'S ANGEL FLAKE** Coconut

6 squares **BAKER'S** Semi-Sweet
   Baking Chocolate, coarsely chopped

1 cup **PLANTERS** Chopped Pecans

1 can (14 ounces) sweetened condensed milk

PREHEAT oven to 350°F. Line 13×9-inch baking pan with foil, with ends of foil extending over sides of pan. Grease foil. Mix butter and cracker crumbs; press firmly onto bottom of prepared pan.

SPRINKLE with coconut, chocolate and pecans; cover with condensed milk.

BAKE 25 to 30 minutes or until golden brown. Cool completely on wire rack. Using foil handles, lift dessert from pan. Cut into 36 bars. Store in tightly covered container at room temperature.

Note: *These quick and easy dessert bars are sure to please any crowd!*   ***Makes 36 servings***

did you know...

German Chocolate Cake did not originate in Germany, but in the U.S.A., at Walter Baker & Company. In 1852, Sam German developed for the company a sweet baking bar that was named in his honor (BAKER'S® GERMAN'S® Sweet Chocolate). One hundred and five years later, a woman in Texas sent a cake recipe using German's Sweet Chocolate to a newspaper in Dallas, causing a spike in the sales of the chocolate variety. Hence, the birth of German Chocolate Cake!

Frozen German Sweet Chocolate Pie

Prep: 20 minutes
Total: 4 hours 30 minutes (includes freezing)

1 package (4 ounces) **BAKER'S GERMAN'S** Sweet Chocolate

⅓ cup milk, divided

4 ounces (½ of 8-ounce package) **PHILADELPHIA** Cream Cheese, softened

2 tablespoons sugar

2 cups thawed **COOL WHIP** Whipped Topping

1 **HONEY MAID** Graham Pie Crust (6-ounce)

Chocolate curls, optional

MICROWAVE chocolate and 2 tablespoons of the milk in large microwaveable bowl on HIGH 1½ to 2 minutes or until chocolate is almost melted, stirring after each minute. Stir until chocolate is completely melted. Add cream cheese, sugar and remaining milk; beat with wire whisk until well blended. Refrigerate 10 minutes to cool.

ADD whipped topping; stir gently until well blended. Spoon into crust.

FREEZE 4 hours or until firm. Let stand at room temperature or in refrigerator about 15 minutes or until pie can be cut easily. Top with chocolate curls before serving, if desired. Store leftover pie in freezer.

Makes 8 servings

  **America's Oldest Chocolate Brand**

Million Dollar Fudge

Prep: 5 minutes • **Total:** 25 minutes

- ½ cup (1 stick) butter or margarine
- 4½ cups sugar
- 1 can (13 ounces) evaporated milk
- 3 packages (12 ounces each) **BAKER'S** Semi-Sweet Chocolate Chunks
- 1 jar (7 ounces) **JET-PUFFED** Marshmallow Creme
- 3 cups **PLANTERS** Chopped Pecans
- 1 teaspoon salt
- 1 teaspoon vanilla

PLACE butter, sugar and milk in heavy 4-quart saucepan. Bring to full rolling boil on medium heat, stirring constantly. Boil 5 minutes, stirring constantly to prevent scorching.

REMOVE from heat. Gradually add chocolate chunks, stirring until chocolate is completely melted. Add remaining ingredients; beat until well blended.

POUR into greased 15×10×1-inch pan. Cool completely. Cut into 60 pieces.

Makes 5 dozen pieces or 60 servings, 1 piece each

*Tip: To make **Rocky Road Fudge,** prepare as directed, stirring 2 cups **JET-PUFFED** Miniature Marshmallows into the hot fudge mixture before pouring into pan.*

Original BAKER'S®
Chocolate Chunk Cookies

Prep: 15 minutes • **Bake:** 12 minutes • **Total:** 27 minutes

1¾ cups flour

¾ teaspoon baking soda

¼ teaspoon salt

¾ cup (1½ sticks) margarine, softened

½ cup granulated sugar

½ cup firmly packed brown sugar

1 egg

1 teaspoon vanilla

1 package (8 squares) **BAKER'S**
  Semi-Sweet Baking Chocolate,
  coarsely chopped

1 cup chopped **PLANTERS** Walnuts

PREHEAT oven to 375°F. Mix flour, baking soda and salt until well blended; set aside.

BEAT margarine and sugars in large bowl with electric mixer on medium speed until light and fluffy. Add egg and vanilla; mix well. Gradually add flour mixture, beating until well blended after each addition. Stir in chopped chocolate and walnuts. Drop heaping tablespoonfuls of dough, 2 inches apart, onto ungreased baking sheets.

BAKE 11 to 12 minutes or until lightly browned. Cool 1 minute; remove from baking sheets to wire racks. Cool completely.

Makes about 3 dozen cookies or 36 servings,
1 cookie each

America's Oldest Chocolate Brand

Wellesley Fudge Cake

Prep: 30 minutes • **Bake:** 35 minutes
Total: 2 hours 5 minutes (includes cooling)

    4 squares **BAKER'S** Unsweetened Baking Chocolate
 1¾ cups sugar, divided
  ½ cup water
 1⅔ cups flour
    1 teaspoon baking soda
  ¼ teaspoon salt
  ½ cup (1 stick) butter or margarine, softened
    3 eggs
  ¾ cup milk
    1 teaspoon vanilla
       Easy Chocolate Frosting (page 85)

PREHEAT oven to 350°F. Microwave chocolate, ½ cup of the sugar and the water in large microwaveable bowl on HIGH 2 minutes or until chocolate is almost melted, stirring after 1 minute. Stir until chocolate is completely melted. Cool to lukewarm.

MIX flour, baking soda and salt; set aside. Beat butter and remaining 1¼ cups sugar in large bowl with electric mixer on medium speed until light and fluffy. Add eggs, 1 at a time, beating well after each addition. Add flour mixture alternately with milk, beating until well blended after each addition. Add chocolate mixture and vanilla; mix well. Pour into 2 greased and floured 9-inch round cake pans.

BAKE 30 to 35 minutes or until toothpick inserted in centers comes out clean. Cool in pans 10 minutes; remove from pans to wire racks. Cool completely. Frost with Easy Chocolate Frosting. ***Makes 16 servings***

  **America's Oldest Chocolate Brand**

White Chocolate Cheesecake

Prep: 35 minutes • **Bake:** 1 hour 30 minutes
Total: 6 hours 5 minutes (includes refrigeration)

¾ cup sugar, divided

½ cup (1 stick) butter or margarine, softened

1½ teaspoons vanilla, divided

1 cup flour

4 packages (8 ounces each) **PHILADELPHIA** Cream Cheese, softened

2 packages (6 squares each) **BAKER'S** Premium White Baking Chocolate, melted and slightly cooled

4 eggs

Raspberries and mint leaves, optional

PREHEAT oven to 325°F if using a silver 9-inch springform pan, or to 300°F if using a dark nonstick 9-inch springform pan. Beat ¼ cup of the sugar, butter and ½ teaspoon of the vanilla in small bowl with electric mixer on medium speed until light and fluffy. Gradually add flour, mixing on low speed until well blended. Press firmly onto bottom of pan; prick with fork. Bake 25 minutes or until edge is lightly browned.

BEAT cream cheese, remaining ½ cup sugar and remaining 1 teaspoon vanilla in large bowl with electric mixer on medium speed until well blended. Add melted chocolate; mix well. Add eggs, 1 at a time, mixing on low speed after each addition just until blended. Pour over crust.

BAKE 55 minutes to 1 hour or until center is almost set. Run knife or metal spatula around rim of pan to loosen cake; cool before removing rim of pan. Refrigerate 4 hours or overnight. Top with raspberries and mint leaf before serving, if desired. Store leftover cheesecake in refrigerator.

Makes 16 servings

Black Bottom Banana Cream Pie

Prep: 30 minutes
Total: 4 hours 30 minutes (includes refrigeration)

  25 **NILLA** Wafers, finely crushed (about 1¼ cups crumbs)

    6 tablespoons butter or margarine, melted, divided

    2 tablespoons sugar

    4 squares **BAKER'S** Semi-Sweet Baking Chocolate

    2 large bananas, sliced

    1 package (4-serving size) **JELL-O** Vanilla Flavor Instant Pudding & Pie Filling

 1¾ cups cold milk

    1 cup thawed **COOL WHIP** Whipped Topping

MIX crumbs, ¼ cup (4 tablespoons) of the melted butter and sugar in medium bowl. Remove 2 tablespoons of the crumb mixture; set aside for later use. Press remaining crumb mixture firmly onto bottom and up side of 9-inch pie plate; set aside.

MICROWAVE chocolate and remaining 2 tablespoons butter in medium microwaveable bowl on HIGH 1 minute or until butter is melted; stir until chocolate is completely melted. Spread evenly onto bottom of crust; top with bananas. Set aside.

PREPARE pudding mix with the 1¾ cups milk as directed on package for pie; pour evenly over bananas. Refrigerate at least 4 hours or overnight. Top with whipped topping just before serving; sprinkle with reserved 2 tablespoons crumb mixture. Store leftover pie in refrigerator.   *Makes 8 servings*

Decadent Triple Layer Mud Pie

Prep: 15 minutes
Total: 3 hours 25 minutes (includes refrigeration)

- 3 squares **BAKER'S** Semi-Sweet Baking Chocolate, melted
- ¼ cup canned sweetened condensed milk
- 1 **OREO** Pie Crust (6-ounce)
- ½ cup chopped **PLANTERS** Pecans, toasted
- 2 cups cold milk
- 2 packages (4-serving size each) **JELL-O** Chocolate Flavor Instant Pudding & Pie Filling
- 1 tub (8 ounces) **COOL WHIP** Whipped Topping, thawed, divided

MIX chocolate and condensed milk until well blended. Pour into crust; sprinkle with pecans.

POUR milk into large bowl. Add dry pudding mixes. Beat with wire whisk 2 minutes or until well blended. (Mixture will be thick.) Spoon 1½ cups of the pudding over pecans in crust. Add half of the whipped topping to remaining pudding; stir with wire whisk until well blended. Spread over pudding layer in crust; top with remaining whipped topping.

REFRIGERATE 3 hours. Store leftover pie in refrigerator.

Makes 10 servings

Tip: To toast nuts, preheat oven to 350°F. Spread pecans in single layer in shallow baking pan. Bake 5 to 7 minutes or until lightly toasted, stirring occasionally. Let cool.

Easy Toasted Coconut Pie

Prep: 10 minutes
Total: 4 hours 10 minutes (includes refrigeration)

    2 squares **BAKER'S** Semi-Sweet Baking Chocolate, chopped
    2 cups thawed **COOL WHIP** Whipped Topping, divided
    ¾ cup **BAKER'S ANGEL FLAKE** Coconut, toasted, divided
    1 **HONEY MAID** Graham Pie Crust (6-ounce)
  1½ cups cold milk
    1 package (4-serving size) **JELL-O** Coconut Cream Flavor Instant Pudding & Pie Filling

MICROWAVE chocolate in medium microwaveable bowl on HIGH 1 minute, stirring after 30 seconds. Stir until chocolate is completely melted. Add 1 cup of the whipped topping and ¼ cup of the coconut; stir until well blended. Spread onto bottom of crust. Refrigerate while preparing filling.

POUR milk into large bowl. Add dry pudding mix. Beat with wire whisk 2 minutes or until well blended. Spoon into crust. Top with remaining 1 cup whipped topping; sprinkle with remaining ½ cup coconut.

REFRIGERATE 4 hours or until ready to serve. Store leftover pie in refrigerator.   *Makes 8 servings*

Tip: To toast coconut, spread **BAKER'S ANGEL FLAKE** Coconut in shallow baking pan. Bake at 350°F for 7 to 10 minutes or until lightly browned, stirring frequently. Or, spread in microwaveable pie plate. Microwave on HIGH 5 minutes or until lightly browned, stirring every 2 minutes.

Mile-High Fudge Brownie Pie

Prep: 25 minutes • **Bake:** 30 minutes
Total: 2 hours 55 minutes (includes refrigeration)

- 4 squares **BAKER'S** Semi-Sweet Baking Chocolate
- ½ cup (1 stick) butter or margarine
- ¾ cup sugar
- 2 eggs
- 1 teaspoon vanilla
- ½ cup flour
- 2 cups cold milk
- 2 packages (4-serving size each) **JELL-O** Chocolate Flavor Instant Pudding & Pie Filling
- 1 tub (8 ounces) **COOL WHIP** Whipped Topping, thawed, divided

PREHEAT oven to 350°F. Microwave chocolate and butter in large microwaveable bowl on HIGH 2 minutes or until butter is melted. Stir until chocolate is completely melted. Add sugar; stir until well blended. Add eggs and vanilla; mix well. Stir in flour until well blended. Spread into greased 9-inch pie plate.

BAKE 30 minutes or until toothpick inserted in center comes out clean. Cool completely on wire rack. Scoop out center of brownie with spoon, leaving ½-inch-thick rim around edge and thin layer of brownie on bottom. Reserve removed brownie pieces.

POUR milk into large bowl. Add dry pudding mixes. Beat with wire whisk 2 minutes or until well blended. (Mixture will be thick.) Gently stir in half of the whipped topping and all but ½ cup of the reserved brownie pieces. Spoon into brownie crust; top with remaining whipped topping and remaining ½ cup brownie pieces. Refrigerate 2 hours or until set. Store leftover pie in refrigerator. *Makes 10 servings*

White Chocolate-Coconut Cream Pie

Prep: 45 minutes • **Bake:** 10 minutes
Total: 4 hours 55 minutes (includes refrigeration)

1½ cups **BAKER'S ANGEL FLAKE** Coconut, divided

4 tablespoons margarine, melted

½ cup **HONEY MAID** Graham Cracker Crumbs

1 package (6 squares) **BAKER'S** Premium White Baking Chocolate, divided

1¾ cups milk

1 package (4-serving size) **JELL-O** Coconut Cream Flavor Instant Pudding & Pie Filling

1½ cups whipping cream, divided

PREHEAT oven to 350°F. Mix 1 cup of the coconut, the margarine and cracker crumbs in 9-inch pie plate. Press firmly onto bottom and up side of pie plate. Bake 10 minutes. Microwave 3 squares of the chocolate in small microwaveable bowl on HIGH 1½ minutes, stirring every 30 seconds. Stir until chocolate is completely melted. Spread onto bottom of crust. Refrigerate 15 minutes, or until chocolate is firm.

POUR milk into large bowl. Add dry pudding mix. Beat with wire whisk 2 minutes or until well blended. Stir in remaining ½ cup coconut; pour into crust. Refrigerate until ready to add next layer. Microwave remaining 3 chocolate squares and ¼ cup of the whipping cream in large microwaveable bowl on HIGH 2 minutes, stirring after 1 minute. Stir until chocolate is completely melted. Cool 20 minutes or until room temperature, stirring occasionally.

BEAT remaining 1¼ cups whipping cream in chilled large bowl with electric mixer on medium-high speed until soft peaks form. Add half of the whipped cream to chocolate mixture; stir until well blended. Gently stir in remaining whipped cream. Spoon over filling in crust. Refrigerate several hours or until chilled. Store leftover pie in refrigerator.

Makes 10 servings

Ultimate Chocolate Caramel Pecan Pie

Prep: 30 minutes • **Bake:** 15 minutes
Total: 3 hours 15 minutes (includes refrigeration)

  3 cups **PLANTERS** Pecan Pieces, divided
  ¼ cup granulated sugar
  ¼ cup (½ stick) butter or margarine, melted
  1 bag (14 ounces) **KRAFT** Caramels
  ⅔ cup whipping cream, divided
  1 package (8 squares) **BAKER'S** Semi-Sweet Baking Chocolate
  ¼ cup powdered sugar
  ½ teaspoon vanilla

PREHEAT oven to 350°F. Place 2 cups of the pecan pieces in food processor or blender container; cover. Process until finely ground, using pulsing action. Mix with granulated sugar and butter. Press firmly onto bottom and up side of 9-inch pie plate. Bake 12 to 15 minutes or until lightly browned. Cool completely. (If crust puffs up during baking, gently press down with back of spoon.)

MICROWAVE caramels and ⅓ cup of the whipping cream in microwaveable bowl on HIGH 2½ to 3 minutes or until caramels are completely melted, stirring after each minute. Pour into crust. Chop remaining 1 cup pecans; sprinkle over caramel layer.

PLACE chocolate, remaining ⅓ cup whipping cream, the powdered sugar and vanilla in saucepan; cook on low heat just until chocolate is completely melted, stirring constantly. Pour over pie; gently spread to evenly cover top of pie. Refrigerate at least 2 hours. Store leftover pie in refrigerator.   ***Makes 10 servings***

Baker's
SINCE 1780

Sweet
Finishing
Touches

Hot Fudge Sauce

Prep: 5 minutes • **Total:** 12 minutes

- 1 package (8 squares) **BAKER'S** Unsweetened Baking Chocolate
- ¼ cup (½ stick) butter or margarine
- ½ cup milk
- ½ cup whipping cream
- 2 cups sugar
- 1 teaspoon vanilla

MICROWAVE chocolate and butter in large microwaveable bowl on HIGH 2 minutes or until butter is melted. Stir until chocolate is completely melted.

ADD milk, whipping cream and sugar; stir until well blended. Microwave 5 minutes or until mixture is thick and sugar is completely dissolved, stirring after 3 minutes. Stir in vanilla. Store in tightly covered container in refrigerator. Reheat just before serving.

Makes 3½ cups or 28 servings,
2 tablespoons each

did you know...

In 1834, 86 years before the 19th Amendment was passed, Walter Baker hired two women to work at the chocolate mill: Mary and Christiana Shields. By 1846, there were several women on the payroll of Walter Baker & Company.

Coconut-Pecan Filling and Frosting

Prep: 5 minutes • **Total:** 17 minutes

    4 egg yolks

    1 can (12 ounces) evaporated milk

1½ teaspoons vanilla

1½ cups sugar

  ¾ cup (1½ sticks) butter or margarine

    1 package (7 ounces) **BAKER'S ANGEL FLAKE** Coconut (about 2⅔ cups)

1½ cups **PLANTERS** Chopped Pecans

BEAT egg yolks, milk and vanilla in large saucepan with wire whisk until well blended. Add sugar and butter; cook on medium heat 12 minutes or until thickened and golden brown, stirring constantly. Remove from heat.

ADD coconut and pecans; mix well. Cool to room temperature or until desired spreading consistency.

USE to frost Original **BAKER'S® GERMAN'S®** Sweet Chocolate Cake (page 18).

Makes 4½ cups or 36 servings, 2 tablespoons each

Tip: This recipe makes enough to frost top and sides of 3 (8- or 9-inch) cake layers, tops of 2 (13×9-inch) cakes or 36 cupcakes.

 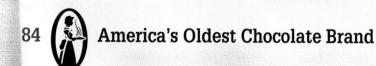

Easy Chocolate Frosting

Prep: 15 minutes • **Total:** 15 minutes

- 4 squares **BAKER'S** Unsweetened Baking Chocolate
- ¼ cup (½ stick) butter or margarine, softened
- 1 package (16 ounces) powdered sugar (about 4 cups), divided
- 1 teaspoon vanilla
- ½ cup milk

MELT chocolate in saucepan on very low heat, stirring constantly; set aside.

BEAT butter in large bowl with electric mixer on medium speed until creamy. Gradually add about half of the powdered sugar, beating on low speed after each addition until well blended. Add chocolate and vanilla; mix well.

ADD remaining sugar alternately with the milk, beating until well blended after each addition. Use to frost Wellesley Fudge Cake (page 66).

Makes 2½ cups or 20 servings, 2 tablespoons each

Tip: *For a variation, substitute 6 squares* ***BAKER'S*** *Semi-Sweet Baking Chocolate for the 4 squares of* ***BAKER'S*** *Unsweetened Baking Chocolate.*

Rich 'N Thick Hot Chocolate

Prep: 5 minutes • **Total:** 10 minutes

1 cup water

2 squares **BAKER'S** Unsweetened Baking Chocolate

½ cup sugar

3 cups milk

1 teaspoon vanilla

JET-PUFFED Miniature Marshmallows, optional

PLACE water and chocolate in heavy medium saucepan; cook on low heat until chocolate is completely melted and mixture is well blended, stirring constantly with wire whisk. Add sugar; mix well.

BRING to boil on medium-high heat. Boil 3 minutes, stirring constantly. Gradually add milk, stirring with wire whisk until well blended. Stir in vanilla. Reduce heat to medium.

COOK until mixture is heated through, stirring occasionally. Serve with marshmallows, if desired.

Makes 4 servings, about 1 cup each

A Rich History

Baker's founder
James Baker

For decades, the familiar orange and red boxes have conjured up memories of home. In the 225 years since Baker's Chocolate was introduced, the product has become a staple—not just in kitchens across the country, but also in the very fabric of American history.

In 1765, Harvard-educated Dr. John Baker met a young Irish immigrant named John Hannon near Boston. Hannon knew how to make a commodity that was growing in popularity in the colonies: chocolate. Dr. Baker decided to finance Hannon, and the two set up shop in a small, wood-framed chocolate mill along the banks of the Neponset River near Boston.

For years, the mill prospered despite several setbacks. In 1775, for example, the original chocolate mill burned to the ground. When the American Revolution began, Baker and Hannon were forced to smuggle shipments of cacao beans through Royal Navy warships in order to continue production. Then, in 1779, Hannon disappeared while on a journey to the West Indies to purchase cacao beans.

Hannon's fateful trip turned out to be the beginning of a legacy that endures today. His widow sold her husband's shares of the business to Dr. Baker, who consolidated operations and established the "Baker's Chocolate Company" in 1780. In doing so, he began producing and selling the first chocolate product with the Baker's name: chocolate cakes used to make a sweetened chocolate drink. He also created a family dynasty that would guide the company for more than a century.

Eleven years after taking over the company, Dr. Baker brought his son, Edmund, into the business and changed the name of the company to "Baker & Son." When Dr. Baker retired in 1804, he entrusted the business solely to Edmund, who opened a new, state-of-the-art chocolate mill.

When Edmund retired in 1824, his son Walter took over and renamed the company "Walter Baker & Company." By 1833, Baker's Chocolate products could be found on the shelves of general stores throughout the young nation, including one co-owned by Abraham Lincoln in Old Salem, IL. As America reached westward, so did distribution of Baker's Chocolate. In fact, in 1849—at the height of the California Gold Rush—Baker's Chocolate and Cocoa were packaged and shipped to the San Francisco area in tin boxes that miners later used to store their gold dust.

1853 advertisement

In 1854, Henry L. Pierce (step-nephew of Walter Baker) took over as head of Walter Baker & Company and guided the company through the trying years of the Civil War. He was the first to market Baker's Chocolate nationally, taking out newspaper advertisements and producing the first Baker's Chocolate cookbook.

After the death of Henry Pierce in 1896, Walter Baker & Company was sold to the Forbes Syndicate. Over the next 30 years, Forbes doubled the size of the Baker's Chocolate complex in Dorchester, Mass.

In 1927, the Forbes Syndicate sold Walter Baker & Company to the Postum Company (later renamed General Foods Corporation). Baker's Chocolate became part of the Kraft Foods portfolio of brands when it merged with General Foods in 1989.

During the past ten years, innovation has kept Baker's Chocolate an integral part of the American kitchen. In the early 1990s, Baker's "One Bowl" Recipes were introduced. These scratch-baked desserts are less time-intensive, thanks to the microwave chocolate-melting technique and efficient use of only one bowl to mix all the ingredients. As the 21st century dawned, consumers got a glimpse into the future of the brand with the introduction of Baker's Dipping Chocolate.

It's hard to believe that what started as a simple partnership on the banks of the Neponset River has become "America's Oldest Chocolate Brand." Though times have changed, one thing is for certain: Baker's Chocolate has helped create many delicious memories over the past 225 years, and will continue to be a staple in sweet treats for years to come.

La Belle Chocolatiere

Gracing each package of Baker's Chocolate products since the 18th Century is the lovely silhouette of La Belle Chocolatiere—the beautiful chocolate waitress. How La Belle came to be on Baker's package is a fairy tale…Once upon a time, a prince visited a Viennese chocolate house where a beautiful young waitress served him. As the tale goes, he fell in love with her and married her. The prince had her portrait painted, and it later hung in the Dresden Museum. In 1813, Henry Pierce, the president of Baker's Chocolate, saw the portrait and was determined that it become a symbol of the company. In 1883, this came to pass, and La Belle Chocolatiere has been the trademark of Baker's Chocolate ever since.

Tips and Techniques

> **Microwave Melting:**

Baker's Semi-Sweet, Unsweetened, Bittersweet or Premium White Baking Chocolate:

Place 1 unwrapped square of Baker's Chocolate in microwaveable bowl. Microwave on HIGH 1 minute or until chocolate is almost melted, stirring after 30 seconds. (When microwaved, chocolate square will retain its shape. Chocolate will continue to melt after being removed from microwave.) Stir 1 minute or until chocolate is completely melted.

If after stirring for 1 minute chocolate is not completely melted, microwave an additional 10 seconds or until only small, unmelted pieces of chocolate remain. Stir until chocolate is completely melted. Repeat if necessary.

For each additional square of chocolate, add 10 seconds to the microwaving time.

Baker's German's Sweet Chocolate:

Unwrap 1 bar of Baker's German's Sweet Chocolate; break in half. Place in microwaveable bowl. Microwave on HIGH 1½ minutes or until chocolate is almost melted, stirring after 1 minute. (When microwaved, chocolate will retain its shape. Chocolate will continue to melt after being removed from microwave.) Stir

1 minute or until chocolate is completely melted.

If after stirring for 1 minute chocolate is not completely melted, microwave an additional 10 seconds or until only small unmelted pieces of chocolate remain. Stir until chocolate is completely melted. Repeat if necessary.

➢ Double Boiler Melting:
Place Baker's Chocolate in top section of double boiler or in heatproof bowl set over a larger pan of simmering, not boiling, water. (Bottom of bowl should not touch the hot water.) Stir occasionally until chocolate is almost melted. Remove from heat; stir until chocolate is completely melted and smooth.

Note: Do not allow any water or steam to get into the melted chocolate. The chocolate will seize, become grainy, and be unusable.

Double Boiler Melting

➢ Stovetop Melting:
Place Baker's Chocolate in small heavy saucepan. Cook on very low heat **just until chocolate is melted**, stirring constantly. Remove from heat; stir until chocolate is completely melted and smooth.

➢ How to Grate Chocolate:
Use the large holes of a hand grater to grate an unwrapped square of room-temperature Baker's Chocolate onto a sheet of wax paper. Use immediately or refrigerate until ready to use.

➢ Storing Chocolate:
Store chocolate in a cool dry place (below 75°F, if possible), but not in the refrigerator. Cocoa butter melts and rises to the surface at higher temperatures. When this happens, the chocolate develops a pale, gray color called "bloom." However, this condition does not affect the chocolate's flavor or quality.

➢ Storing Chocolate Garnishes:
Grated chocolate, chocolate curls, leaves, or cutouts can be stored in an airtight container in the freezer up to 6 months.

Chocolate Drizzle

➤ **Chocolate Drizzle:**
Melt Baker's Chocolate as directed on package. Use a small spoon to drizzle melted chocolate over desserts. Or, spoon melted chocolate into a small resealable plastic bag; seal bag. Cut a tiny piece (about ⅛-inch) off 1 of the bottom corners of bag. Drizzle chocolate over desserts as desired.

➤ **How to Make Chocolate Curls:**
Melt 4 squares Baker's Semi-Sweet or Premium White Baking Chocolate or 1 package (4 ounces) Baker's German's Sweet Chocolate as directed on package. Spread with spatula into a very thin layer on baking sheet. Refrigerate 10 minutes, or until chocolate is firm but still pliable.

To make curls, push a metal spatula firmly along the baking sheet under the chocolate so the chocolate curls as it is pushed. (The width of the curls will vary depending on the width of the spatula.)

If chocolate is too firm to curl, let stand a few minutes at room temperature; refrigerate again if it becomes too soft.

Use a toothpick to place chocolate curl onto a sheet of wax paper. Use immediately or refrigerate until ready to use. Use toothpick to arrange curls on dessert.

➤ **Alternative Peeler Method:**
Warm 1 wrapped square of Baker's Chocolate in your hand. Pull a vegetable peeler across the surface of the unwrapped chocolate, allowing shavings to fall onto a sheet of wax paper. Use immediately or refrigerate until ready to use.

Index

Notes

METRIC CONVERSION CHART

VOLUME MEASUREMENTS (dry)

⅛ teaspoon = 0.5 mL
¼ teaspoon = 1 mL
½ teaspoon = 2 mL
¾ teaspoon = 4 mL
1 teaspoon = 5 mL
1 tablespoon = 15 mL
2 tablespoons = 30 mL
¼ cup = 60 mL
⅓ cup = 75 mL
½ cup = 125 mL
⅔ cup = 150 mL
¾ cup = 175 mL
1 cup = 250 mL
2 cups = 1 pint = 500 mL
3 cups = 750 mL
4 cups = 1 quart = 1 L

VOLUME MEASUREMENTS (fluid)

1 fluid ounce (2 tablespoons) = 30 mL
4 fluid ounces (½ cup) = 125 mL
8 fluid ounces (1 cup) = 250 mL
12 fluid ounces (1½ cups) = 375 mL
16 fluid ounces (2 cups) = 500 mL

WEIGHTS (mass)

½ ounce = 15 g
1 ounce = 30 g
3 ounces = 90 g
4 ounces = 120 g
8 ounces = 225 g
10 ounces = 285 g
12 ounces = 360 g
16 ounces = 1 pound = 450 g

DIMENSIONS

1/16 inch = 2 mm
⅛ inch = 3 mm
¼ inch = 6 mm
½ inch = 1.5 cm
¾ inch = 2 cm
1 inch = 2.5 cm

OVEN TEMPERATURES

250°F = 120°C
275°F = 140°C
300°F = 150°C
325°F = 160°C
350°F = 180°C
375°F = 190°C
400°F = 200°C
425°F = 220°C
450°F = 230°C

BAKING PAN SIZES

Utensil	Size in Inches/Quarts	Metric Volume	Size in Centimeters
Baking or Cake Pan (square or rectangular)	8×8×2	2 L	20×20×5
	9×9×2	2.5 L	23×23×5
	12×8×2	3 L	30×20×5
	13×9×2	3.5 L	33×23×5
Loaf Pan	8×4×3	1.5 L	20×10×7
	9×5×3	2 L	23×13×7
Round Layer Cake Pan	8×1½	1.2 L	20×4
	9×1½	1.5 L	23×4
Pie Plate	8×1¼	750 mL	20×3
	9×1¼	1 L	23×3
Baking Dish or Casserole	1 quart	1 L	—
	1½ quart	1.5 L	—
	2 quart	2 L	—